Memory-Boosting
Mnemonic Songs
for Content Area Learning

Meish Goldish

NEW YORK • TORONTO • LONDON • AUCKLAND • SYDNEY
MEXICO CITY • NEW DELHI • HONG KONG • BUENOS AIRES

Teaching
Resources

Cover design by Lillian Kohli
Interior design by Melinda Belter
Interior illustrations by Mike Moran

ISBN-13 978-0-439-60306-5
ISBN-10 0-439-60306-4

Contents

LANGUAGE ARTS

SOCIAL STUDIES

MATH & SCIENCE

Introduction

Turn to the mnemonic songs in this collection to help students learn essential information—information they'll need time and time again both inside and outside the classroom.

Each song has been written with students in grades 3–6 in mind and complements key curriculum areas in language arts, science, math, and social studies. The engaging lyrics, containing vital facts and concepts, are set to familiar tunes such as "Camptown Races," "Alouette," and "This Land Is Your Land."

You'll soon discover that teaching with mnemonic songs, in addition to providing a motivating learning context, is a powerful approach you can use to help students recall, remember, and ultimately master important information. So, have fun! Hear how music can make learning stick!

HOW TO USE THE SONGS

Before you introduce a mnemonic song to the class, help students think about how music can be a valuable learning tool. Invite volunteers to name or sing songs they've committed to memory in order to recall information. You might explain that the class will be learning mnemonic songs, with lyrics written specifically to bolster what students are learning in the classroom.

Once you've selected a mnemonic song for students to learn, you may choose to present it in a variety of ways. Here are three suggestions to get you started:

Research Based
Using familiar tunes as mnemonic devices is an effective learning strategy that can help students of all abilities.

Scaffold Learning
A mnemonic device provides a structure for learning or acquiring information, a series of organizing factors to ensure durable retention, and effective cues for retrieval of the memorized information (Ashcraft, 1989, pp.195–196).

Improve Performance
"Memory as it interacts with mastery of educational content is an important process which affects academic success" (Gfeller, 1982, p. 5).

Construct Knowledge
"For many LD students, mnemonic instruction may represent the only realistic chance they will comprehend specific academic content . . ." (Scruggs and Mastropieri, 1990, p. 277).

- Provide a copy of the song to each student. Invite volunteers to hum the first verse or the chorus to help familiarize the class with the tune. Then, as a group, clap or tap out the rhythm. When the class is ready, sing the first verse aloud. Invite volunteers to examine the lyrics in each verse, pointing out key vocabulary and concepts. As a group, learn and practice singing the song together.

- Give a copy of the song lyrics to each student. Read the song lyrics through, as a class. Invite volunteers to talk about how the song lyrics connect to topics the class is studying. (For example, you might invite volunteers to draw comparisons between events described in a textbook and the same events described by the lyrics.) Then, during class time, have students work in small groups to reread the lyrics, recall the tune, and sing the mnemonic song together.

- Reacquaint students with the tune, by humming aloud for the class and inviting students to join in when they are ready. If you prefer, play the tune on an instrument such as a kazoo. Or, if you have a computer with speakers in your classroom, play the tune from a music Web site, such as one of the ones listed at right. Next, provide each student with a photocopy of the song. As a group, read the lyrics aloud. Take time to introduce unfamiliar vocabulary and concepts.

Helpful Web Sites

www.songwritershalloffame.org The National Academy of Popular Music Songwriters Hall of Fame Virtual Museum offers visitors unparalleled access to photos, biographies, song lists, audio clips, and much more.

www.niehs.nih.gov/kids/music.htm Provided by the National Institute of Environmental Health Sciences, the NIEHS Kids' Pages Web site features an extensive database of song lyrics and free downloads for children, parents, and educators.

www.kididdles.com This Web site, the innovation of a mother with a passion for music, is a treasure trove of children's song lyrics and audio clips.

Remember that the goal is to help students draw on songs as mnemonic devices. To help students retain the lyrics—the facts and ideas you want them to learn—set aside time a few days a week for students to practice, practice, practice. They can rehearse as a whole class, in small groups, in pairs, or individually.

"A vital part of the music, movement, and learning connection is the realization we are all songwriters."

—Hap Palmer

TEACHING ACTIVITIES

Boost students' learning of mnemonic songs—and the information contained within them—with the following ideas.

Same Tune, New Verse

Ask students to use their knowledge of the curriculum topic the class is studying to make up a new verse for a mnemonic song you've selected. Divide the class into small groups. Give each group a copy of the mnemonic song. Then explain that you'd like each group to write one more verse for the song. Have students use the song's first verse as a guide for writing their new verse. Later, invite each group to sing its verse for the class.

Having students create their own verses has many benefits, including:

- making learning motivating, personal, and meaningful

- providing opportunities for students to demonstrate knowledge and show relationships between facts and causes and effects

- supporting creativity and strengthening self-esteem

Locked-On to Learning

Strengthen students' grasp of the lyrics through visualization, a comprehension strategy that involves creating mental images based on what we've heard or read. Begin by distributing drawing paper to students. Have each student fold his or her paper in half, turn the page, and then fold it in half again. When unfolded, the paper should have four sections. Ask students to number the sections 1 through 4, then flip the page over and number those sections 5 though 8. Explain that as you read the lyrics aloud, you'll stop reading at the end of each verse and after the initial chorus. Each time, you'll ask students to draw a picture in one of the boxes. The drawings should depict the facts or events from the song.

When students are ready, read or sing the first verse and stop. Ask students to draw a picture that shows what's happening. To check for comprehension, you may want to ask for volunteers and have them describe their drawings. You can also observe what individual students draw and invite them to explain their illustrations. For example, after listening to the third verse of "Systems of the Human Body," one student might draw a person jogging next to a drawing of a flexing bicep. After the drawings are complete, provide each student with a copy of the lyrics. Have students number the verses and then compare his or her illustrations to the lyrics. As a group, discuss the drawings. Encourage students to talk about some of the ways in which visualizing can strengthen connections and make remembering the information in the songs even easier.

♪ Take It on the Road!

Wrap up a unit of study by having students perform some of the mnemonic songs they've learned, reinforcing their newfound knowledge. As a group, talk about the various topics that the songs covered.

Break the class into small groups and assign each group one of the songs to perform for the rest of the class. Encourage groups to embellish their presentations by playing musical instruments, donning costumes, dramatizing lyrics through movement and dance, and so on. In the days ahead, you can help groups adequately prepare for the big day by allowing ample class time for rehearsals. You might even consider having groups perform their songs for younger children in the school—introducing those children to important content, while celebrating the learning that's been taking place in your classroom. Finally, make an audio or video recording of each group's performance. You'll have one more way of assessing student learning and, if you make a few copies to lend, students will have an exciting way of sharing their experiences with their families.

Further Reading

To learn more about the benefits of using music as a multi-sensory approach to teaching, look for articles on the subject. You might begin with reading:

• Gfeller, K. (1983). Musical mnemonics as an aid to retention with normal and learning disabled students. *Journal of Music Therapy, 20*(4), 179–189.

• Kilgour, A. R., Jakobson, L. S., and Cuddy, L. L. (2000). Music training and rate of presentation as mediators of text and song recall. *Memory & Cognition*, 28(5), 700–710.

• Wallace, W. (1994). Memory for music: effect of melody on recall of text. *Learning, Memory, and Cognition*, 20(6), 1471–1485.

References

Ashcraft, M. H. (1989). *Human memory and cognition*. New York: HarperCollins

Gfeller, K. E. (1982). The use of melodic-rhythmic mnemonics with learning disabled and normal students as an aid to retention (Doctoral dissertation, Michigan State University). *University Microfilms International,* No. 8303786.

Scruggs, T. E., and Mastropieri, M. A. (1990). Mnemonic instruction for students with learning disabilities: What it is and what it does. *Learning Disability Quarterly, 13,* 271–279.

LANGUAGE ARTS

Eight Parts of Speech

(sung to "Alouette")

Chorus:
Parts of speech,
Eight parts of speech.
Parts of speech,
Oh, tell me what they are!

Noun names person, place, or thing:
Doctor, office, school, or *ring,*
Place or thing, *school* or *ring,*
O-o-o-o-oh!

Chorus

Pronoun takes the place of noun:
She for *queen,* and *it* for *town,*
Place of noun, *it* for *town,*
O-o-o-o-oh!

Chorus

Verb names action happening:
Eat and *run* and *dance* and *sing,*
Happening, *dance* and *sing,*
O-o-o-o-oh!

Chorus

Adjective describes a noun:
Silly, noisy, happy clown,
Describes a noun, *happy* clown,
O-o-o-o-oh!

Chorus

Adverb modifies a verb:
Listen *well,* do *not* disturb!
Modifies a verb, do *not* disturb!
O-o-o-o-oh!

Chorus

Preposition shows relation:
In the car lot *near* the station,
Shows relation, *near* the station,
O-o-o-o-oh!

Chorus

Conjunction joins two separate words:
Cold *and* snowy, fish *or* birds,
Separate words, fish *or* birds,
O-o-o-o-oh!

Chorus

Interjection shows surprise:
Oh, my dear! Gee whiz! How wise!
Shows surprise. *Gee, how wise!*
O-o-o-o-oh!

Chorus

Nouns

(sung to "London Bridge")

There are many kinds of nouns,
Kinds of nouns, kinds of nouns.
There are many kinds of nouns.
Now let's name them!

Common nouns are general names:
Doctor, friend, theater, games.
What makes all these nouns the same?
All are common.

Proper nouns are special names:
Oakdale Road, Doctor Ames.
What makes all these nouns the same?
All are proper.

Concrete nouns you feel and see:
Office, cup, bumblebee.
A noun that names what you can see
Must be concrete.

Abstract nouns are qualities.
Things you can't touch or see:
Kindness, love, democracy.
These are abstract.

Collective nouns name a group:
Class or *club*, that's a group.
Orchestra names a group.
That's collective.

Compound nouns are two words joined:
Baseball, daydream, tenderloin.
A noun made up of two words joined
Must be compound.

Singular nouns name just one thing:
Actor, shoe, picture, ring.
A noun that names just one thing
Must be singular.

Plural nouns name two or more:
Teachers, homes, women, stores.
A noun that names two or more
Must be plural.

Pronouns

(sung to "You Are My Sunshine")

I know my pronouns,
So many pronouns,
Words that can be used
In place of nouns.
If you know pronouns
Like I know pronouns,
You will see just how many
Can be found.

Personal pronouns
Refer to people:
I, you, she, he, it,
Me, we, and *they*.
Of course, remember:
Him, her, us, and *them*.
Those are all personal pronouns
You say.

Possessive pronouns
Show who's the owner:
My, mine, your, yours,
Her, hers, or *his*.
Of course, remember:
Its, ours, and *theirs*.
Possessive pronouns
Show whose it is.

Indefinite pronouns
Are somewhat general:
Anyone or *someone*,
All or *none*,
Several or *many*,
Both or *neither*.
Indefinite pronouns
Are good for *everyone*.

Demonstrative pronouns
Are more specific.
They're for specific
People, places, things:
Like *this* and *that*,
And *these* and *those*.
Demonstrative pronouns
Point to specific things.

Reflexive pronouns
Refer back to subjects:
Myself, yourself,
Himself, herself,
Itself, ourselves,
Yourselves, themselves.
Reflexive pronouns
Speak for *themselves*.

Intensive pronouns
Are all reflexive.
They stress a noun or
A pronoun well:
The mayor *himself*,
We *ourselves*.
Intensive pronouns
Stress subjects very well.

Interrogative pronouns
All ask a question:
What, which, or *who*,
Whom or *whose*?
When you are starting
To ask a question,
Which interrogative pronoun
Will you use?

Verbs

(sung to "Eensy Weensy Spider")

An action verb names action:
Maria *sings* a song.
A linking verb is being:
Maria's song *is* long.
A helping verb helps main verbs:
Maria *has* begun.
The infinitive form uses *to*:
To sing a song is fun.

The tense of a verb
Shows when action takes place.
Past tense was before:
A cat *washed* its face.
Present tense happens now:
A dog *sees* the cat.
Future tense is yet to come:
The cat *will run* like that.

Regular verbs
Change to past with *-ed*:
I *work* in a classroom.
I *worked* until three.
Irregular verbs
Change to past in other ways:
I *have* a bad cold.
I *had* it seven days.

Adjectives That Compare

(sung to "Three Blind Mice")

Chorus:
Adjectives
That compare
Have three forms
That compare:

Positive describes a thing.
Comparative compares two things.
Superlative compares all things.
Adjectives.

Chorus

Positive: Paul is *tall*.
Comparative: I'm *taller* than Paul.
Superlative: She's *tallest* of all.
Adjectives.

Chorus

Positive: Paul had a *bad* cold.
Comparative: Mine was *worse* than Paul's.
Superlative: Hers was *worst* of all.
Adjectives.

Chorus

Positive: Paul owns a *good* ball.
Comparative: Mine is *better* than Paul's.
Superlative: Hers is *best* of all.
Adjectives.

Synonyms

(sung to "Sing a Song of Sixpence")

Sing a song of synonyms: *tiny* and *small*,
Instantly and *quickly*, *towering* and *tall*,
Difficult and *hard*, *arrived* and *came*.
Synonyms are different words whose meanings are the same.

Sing a song of synonyms: *simple* and *plain*,
Mysterious and *strange*, *shower* and *rain*,
Amazing and *remarkable*, *object* and *aim*.
Synonyms are different words whose meanings are the same.

Sing a song of synonyms: *melody* and *tune*,
Intelligent and *smart*, *clown* and *buffoon*,
Demonstrate and *show*, *fire* and *flame*.
Synonyms are different words whose meanings are the same.

Antonyms

(sung to "Mary Had a Little Lamb")

Pairs of words are antonyms,
Antonyms, antonyms.
Pairs of words are antonyms
When they're the opposite.

Buy and *sell* are antonyms.
Sick and *well* are antonyms.
Rose and *fell* are antonyms.
They mean the opposite.

Start and *end* are antonyms.
Rip and *mend* are antonyms.
Foe and *friend* are antonyms.
They mean the opposite.

Off and *on* are antonyms.
Here and *gone* are antonyms.
Pro and *con* are antonyms.
They mean the opposite.

Work and *rest* are antonyms.
Worst and *best* are antonyms.
Host and *guest* are antonyms.
They mean the opposite.

Give and *take* are antonyms.
Real and *fake* are antonyms.
Fix and *break* are antonyms.
They mean the opposite.

Shrank and *grew* are antonyms.
Old and *new* are antonyms.
Caught and *threw* are antonyms.
They mean the opposite.

Dull and *bright* are antonyms.
Wrong and *right* are antonyms.
Loose and *tight* are antonyms.
They mean the opposite.

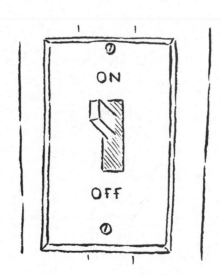

Homonyms

(sung to "Little Brown Jug")

Chorus:
To, two, too,
So, sew, sow,
How many homonyms do you know?
To, two, too,
By, buy, bye,
How many homonyms can you spy?

I *ate* bread at *eight* o'clock.
In one *hour*, *our* ship will dock.
Do you *write* with your *right* hand?
Let's stay *here* and *hear* the band!

Chorus

Pairs of *pears* are what I like.
The *brake* may *break* on my old bike.
A storm *blew* on the deep *blue* sea.
I've *seen* a *scene* that's new to me.

Chorus

The new bus *fare* seems *fair* to me.
Along the shore, you *see* the *sea*.
A *hare* has *hair* that's soft and dry.
Is there a *way* to *weigh* a fly?

Chorus

I felt *weak* one day last *week*.
Do birds get *dew* upon their beak?
We *rode* a tractor on the *road*.
I *sent* you every *cent* I owed.

Chorus

We *heard* mooing from the *herd*.
I *read* about a strange *red* bird.
We *passed* your house at half *past* ten.
I will blink my *eye* again.

Chorus

Prefixes

(sung to "The Muffin Man")

Chorus:
Do you know your prefixes,
Your prefixes, your prefixes?
Do you know your prefixes?
A prefix starts a word.

un- means "not" as in *unknown.*
re- means "again" as in *resewn.*
co- means "with" as in *co-own.*
A prefix starts a word.

Chorus

pre- means "before" as in *preheat.*
semi- means "part" as in *semisweet.*
in- means "not" as in *incomplete.*
A prefix starts a word.

Chorus

dis- means "from" as in *dislocate.*
inter- means "between" as in *interstate.*
circum- means "around" as in *circumnavigate.*
A prefix starts a word.

Chorus

fore- means "front" as in *forehead.*
mis- means "wrong" as in *misled.*
sub- means "under" as in *subhead.*
A prefix starts a word.

Chorus

dis- means "not" as is *disagree.*
fore- means "before" as in *foresee.*
il- means "not" as in *illegally.*
A prefix starts a word.

Chorus

Suffixes

(sung to "Hush, Little Baby")

Look very closely at words, my friend,
You may find a suffix attached to the end:

-ful means "full of" as in *hopeful*.
-able means "can be" as in *loveable*.

-less means "without" as in *careless*.
-ness means "the state of" as in *happiness*.

-or means "one who" as in *actor*.
-ward means "direction of" as in *skyward*.

-ly means "like" as in *kingly*.
-y means "having" as in *itchy*.

-ous means "full of" as in *dangerous*.
-ess means "female" as in *lioness*.

-ic means "like" as in *angelic*.
-fic means "causing" as in *terrific*.

-ment means "the act of" as in *movement*.
-en means "to make" as in *darken*.

-ist means "one who" as in *typist*.
-ish means "resembling" as in *goldish*.

Look very closely at words, my friend,
You may find a suffix attached to the end.

Scholastic Teaching Resources

Four Types of Sentences

(sung to "Down by the Station")

Declarative sentences
All make a statement:
I visited my cousin.
Clouds are in the sky.

Declarative sentences
All make a statement:
Today is Friday.
We hope to bake a pie.

Interrogative sentences
All ask a question:
Where is your raincoat?
Do you know the time?

Interrogative sentences
All ask a question:
When will the game start?
Did you lose a dime?

Imperative sentences
All give an order:
Open the door, please.
Stay here a while.

Imperative sentences
All give an order:
Please call him later.
Look at me and smile.

Exclamatory sentences
Express strong emotion:
Wow! That's amazing!
Thanks! You're a dear!

Exclamatory sentences
Express strong emotion:
What a great story!
I can't believe you're here!

Parts of a Sentence

(sung to "The Mulberry Bush")

Chorus:
In a sentence, you will get
A subject and a predicate.
A subject and a predicate
Join to make a sentence.

A subject has a pronoun or noun
That tells who the sentence is about:
The happy crowd began to shout.
The happy crowd is the subject.

Chorus

A predicate includes a verb
That tells of the subject in one or more words:
The noisy crowd could be heard.
Could be heard is the predicate.

Chorus

Punctuation Marks

(sung to "Clementine")

Punctuation, punctuation,
Punctuation marks to choose.
When it comes to punctuation,
Do you know which marks to use?

Use a period (.) to end a statement:
Apples make a healthy snack.
Use a question mark (?) to end a question:
When will you be coming back?

An exclamation point (!) shows emotion:
Hip hooray! That's really swell!
Use quotation marks (" ") around words spoken:
Doctor Jones said, "You are well."

An apostrophe (') shows possession:
Take a look at Jerry's drums.
Use a comma (,) to separate items:
I like peaches, pears, and plums.

Use a colon (:) before a list:
I've three friends: Jim, Pat, and Mike.
Use ellipsis (. . .) to show what's missing:
A's for apple, B's for bike . . .

Capitalization

(sung to "Auld Lang Syne")

When you are writing sentences,
The first letter's capitalized.
When you are writing sentences,
You must always capitalize.

Today is cold. My soup is hot.
His sister won a prize.
When you are writing sentences,
You must always capitalize.

When you are writing proper nouns,
The first letter's capitalized.
When you are writing proper nouns,
You must always capitalize.

Professor Hill, November 1,
The *Missouri Compromise.*
When you are writing proper nouns,
You must always capitalize.

When you write proper adjectives,
The first letter's capitalized.
When you write proper adjectives,
You must always capitalize.

An *English* muffin, or *French* toast,
Or clear *Alaskan* skies.
When you write proper adjectives,
You must always capitalize.

26

Types of Stories

(sung to "Alouette")

Chorus:
Types of stories,
Different types of stories,
Types of stories
For you to read and write.

Fiction stories aren't true:
Myth and legend, to name two.
Fables, too, aren't true.
O-o-o-o-oh!

Chorus

Romance, mystery, and tall tale;
These are fiction works as well.
Fairy tale? False as well.
O-o-o-o-oh!

Chorus

Science fiction, allegory;
Each one is a made-up story.
Allegory? Made-up story.
O-o-o-o-oh!

Chorus

Fantasy and horror tale;
These are fiction works as well.
Many fiction works to tell.
O-o-o-o-oh!

Chorus

Other stories are all true.
They're nonfiction, just for you.
Essay, journal; to name two.
O-o-o-o-oh!

Chorus

Biography, autobiography;
Both are true as they can be.
Also true? History.
O-o-o-o-oh!

Chorus

Scholastic Teaching Resources

Parts of a Story

(sung to "Bingo")

I know a story has four parts.
Four parts make up a story.

Chorus:
Four main story parts,
Four main story parts,
Four main story parts,
Four parts to every story.

The plot is all the action
Taking place throughout the story.

Chorus

The characters are people
Taking part in all the action.

Chorus

The setting is the time and place
In which the story happens.

Chorus

The theme's the lesson that you learn
By the story's ending.

Chorus

Parts of a Poem

(sung to "Oh Where, Oh Where Has My Little Dog Gone?")

Chorus:
Oh what, oh what does a poem include?
Oh what, oh what does it need?
What are things to do when you're writing a poem,
Or things to note as you read?

A poem will often have some words that rhyme.
Their ending sounds are the same.
When you read a poem, see if some words may rhyme,
Like *aim, came, name,* and *exclaim.*

Chorus

Some poems have rhythm—a good, steady beat,
Repeating time and again.
When rhythm is made by the syllables stressed,
Meter is what it's called then.

Chorus

In alliteration, the same sound repeats
At the beginning of words:
Six sleepy sailors sailed on seven seas.
How often the *s* sound is heard.

Chorus

With onomatopoeia, the words that are used
Sound like the things that they name.
With a *boom*, a *zip*, a *gargle*, or *rip*;
Each word and sound is the same.

Chorus

The imagery in a poem is key.
Words form a scene mentally:
Foamy white waves crashed the sandy beach.
That picture's easy to see.

Chorus

Similes and Metaphors

(sung to "Oh, Dear! What Can the Matter Be?")

Tell me! What is a simile?
It compares two different things.
And be aware that a simile
Uses the word *like* or *as*.

The teenager's height shot up *like* a rocket.
Her smile was *as* bright *as* a shiny, new locket.
Our house is *as* quiet *as* an empty pants pocket.
All similes use *like* or *as*.

Tell me, what is a metaphor?
It compares two things, for sure.
But be aware that a metaphor
Hasn't the word *like* or *as*.

His arms are machines that never stop going.
The poet's sweet words are gentle and flowing.
The team has a spirit so warm and glowing.
No metaphors have *like* or *as*.

Personification

(sung to "On Top of Old Smoky")

Personification,
Now, that would mean what?
To make something human
When really it's not.

The flower was dancing.
The sun smiled at me.
Personification
Is what that would be.

The north wind was laughing.
The moon beamed with glee.
Personification
Is what that would be.

The day dragged on slowly.
My heart leapt so free.
Personification
Is what that would be.

Personification,
Now, that would mean what?
To make something human
When really it's not.

The Writing Process

(sung to "Hokey Pokey")

You start to brainstorm first,
You start to get ideas.
You start to brainstorm first,
To choose what your topic is.

Chorus:
Use the writing process
Whenever you compose.
That's what it's all about!

You do a rough first draft,
You get your thoughts down fast.
You do a rough first draft,
Though it will not be your last.

Chorus

You then revise your work,
You change your words some more.
You then revise your work,
So it's better than before.

Chorus

You proofread all you wrote,
You hunt for each mistake.
You proofread all you wrote,
And correct the slips you make.

Chorus

You do a final draft,
You write it perfectly.
You do a final draft
That's as good as it can be.

Chorus

You publish what you wrote.
You share your work. Oh boy!
You publish what you wrote
For your readers to enjoy.

Chorus

Writing a Paragraph

(sung to "Pussycat, Pussycat")

Paragraph, paragraph,
What can it be?
One group of sentences
About one idea.
Paragraph, paragraph,
What does it say?
It covers the topic
In an organized way.

Paragraph, paragraph,
What do I see?
One topic sentence
With the main idea.
Paragraph, paragraph,
What does it say?
It states the idea
In a brief and clear way.

Paragraph, paragraph,
What more's in store?
Some detail sentences
To give support.
Paragraph, paragraph,
What do they do?
Explain the idea
In more detail for you.

Provide Details!

(sung to "Camptown Races")

When you write, be sure to give
Details! Details!
Make descriptions creative
With details all around!
Say exactly what you mean!
Details! Details!
You can really set the scene
With details all around!

Chorus:
How does something look,
Feel, smell, taste, or sound?
Make descriptions come alive
With details all around!

Don't just write *There was a man.*
Details! Details!
Paint the man as best you can
With details all around!
A strong and healthy man was he.
Details! Details!
His hair was red as strawberries.
Details all around!

Chorus

Don't just write *I got a bike.*
Details! Details!
Tell exactly what it's like
With details all around!
My bike is shiny black and blue.
Details! Details!
The seat is high and feels soft, too.
Details all around!

Chorus

34

Avoid Tired Words!

(sung to "Do Your Ears Hang Low?")

Do the words you choose
Tend to be overused?
Do the words you write
Sound plain and trite?
Are the words you find
Of an ordinary kind?
Then avoid tired words!

Don't always use *said*.
Be more colorful instead!
Write *muttered* or *shouted*
Or *announced* or *pled*.
Use *claimed* or *exclaimed*
Instead of *said*.
Yes, avoid tired words!

Don't always use *went*,
Find a word that's different!
Write *strutted* or *loped*
To tell how he went.
Use *strolled* or *rolled*
Instead of *went*.
Yes, avoid tired words!

Don't always use *looked*.
That word is overcooked!
Write *peeked* or *spied*
Or *gazed* or *eyed*.
Use *stared* or *glared*
Instead of *looked*.
Yes, avoid tired words!

Compare and Contrast

(sung to "The Old Gray Mare")

When you compare
How two things are similar,
Two things are similar,
Two things are similar,
When you compare
How two things are similar,
Show how they're both the same!

Show how they're both the same!
Show how they're both the same!

When you contrast
How two things are different,
Two things are different,
Two things are different,
When you contrast
How two things are different,
Show how they're not the same!

Show how they're not the same!
Show how they're not the same!

When you write, you might
Compare or contrast a lot,
Compare or contrast a lot,
Compare or contrast a lot.
When you write, you might
Compare or contrast a lot
How things are the same or not!

Hard-to-Spell Words

(sung to "The Farmer in the Dell")

Some words are hard to spell.
Some words are hard to spell.
Study how each word is spelled
And learn the spelling well!

Chief and *broccoli*,
Debt and *guarantee*,
License, laugh, corduroy, and *half*;
Some words are hard to spell.

Cantaloupe, surprise,
Committee, exercise,
Guess, proceed, gauge, precede;
Some words are hard to spell.

Nuisance, vaccinate,
Business, separate,
Comb, address, excel, excess;
Some words are hard to spell.

Obedience and *league,*
Glacier and *fatigue,*
Mathematics, independence;
Some words are hard to spell.

Environment, misspell,
Potatoes, parallel,
Wednesday, eighth, kindergarten;
Some words are hard to spell.

Judgment, counterfeit,
Conscience, definite,
Already, truly, caterpillar;
Some words are hard to spell.

Cinnamon, acquire,
Environment, sapphire,
Mattress, height, a lot, all right;
Some words are hard to spell.

Beauty, Antarctic,
Often, arithmetic,
Rhythm, asthma, prairie, plasma;
Some words are hard to spell.

Formerly, fascinate,
Enough, exaggerate,
Cemetery, February;
Some words are hard to spell.

Mosquitoes and *receipt,*
Tomatoes, crumb, and *suite,*
Probably, raspberry;
Some words are hard to spell.

SOCIAL STUDIES

Seven Continents

(sung to "This Land Is Your Land")

A giant land mass
Is called a continent.
And in our vast world
Are seven continents.
If you want to name
The seven continents,
Simply recall the letter A.

A is for Asia.
A is for Africa.
A for Australia.
A for Antarctica.
A for two Americas:
North and South America,
Plus Europe,
That's seven continents.

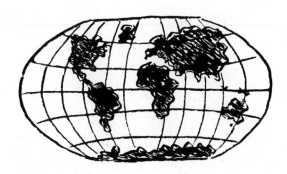

Rivers and Mountains

(sung to "Over the River and Through the Wood")

Look at the rivers around the world!
Some major ones that flow:
The Nile, Amazon, and Yangtze,
The Congo and Huang Ho.
Look at the rivers around the world!
Some major ones to view:
The Niger, Mekong, Mississippi,
Missouri, and Volga, too.

Look at the mountains around the world!
Some major ones that rise:
McKinley, Everest, Kilimanjaro,
K2—all great in size.
Look at the mountains around the world!
Some major ones to see:
Pikes Peak, Matterhorn, Mauna Loa,
Rainier, and Fuji.

42

Greek Gods

(sung to "My Bonnie Lies Over the Ocean")

Poseidon was god of the ocean
And Ares was god over war.
Athena was goddess of wisdom.
These gods ancient Greeks did adore.

Chorus:
Greek gods, Greek gods,
The rulers in old Greek mythology,
Greek gods, Greek gods,
The rulers in mythology.

Artemis was goddess of hunting.
Apollo was god over light
And Hermes protected all travelers.
Each god possessed powerful might.

Chorus

Hypnos was god over sleeping
And Eros was god over love.
The goddess of marriage was Hera,
Upon Mount Olympus above.

Chorus

The goddess of plants was Demeter.
The god of the forest was Pan.
The love goddess was Aphrodite.
The spreading of love was her plan.

Chorus

The underworld ruler was Hades.
The ruler of all gods was Zeus.
Adored by the ancient Greek people
From Athens to old Syracuse.

Chorus

Roman Gods

(sung to "Polly Wolly Doodle")

Cupid was the god of love
In Roman mythology.
Neptune was the god of the sea
In Roman mythology.

Venus was the goddess of love
In Roman mythology.
Mars was the god of war
In Roman mythology.

Chorus:
How they ruled, how they ruled,
How they ruled so powerfully!
On the hills of Rome
Gods made their home
In Roman mythology.

Vulcan was the god of fire
In Roman mythology.
Diana was the goddess of the moon
In Roman mythology.

Somnus was the god of sleep
In Roman mythology.
Juno was the queen of the gods
In Roman mythology.

Chorus

Janus guarded doors and gates
In Roman mythology.
Mercury protected travelers
In Roman mythology.

Minerva was the goddess of wisdom
In Roman mythology.
Ceres was the goddess of growth
In Roman mythology.

Chorus

Apollo was the god of light
In Roman mythology.
Saturn was the god of crops
In Roman mythology.

Pluto ruled the underworld
In Roman mythology.
And Jupiter ruled over *all* the gods
In Roman mythology.

Chorus

Ancient Egypt

(sung to "Eensy Weensy Spider")

Back in ancient Egypt
The people farmed in style,
Irrigating land with
Water from the Nile,
Planting lots of barley
And vegetables and wheat,
And despite the arid setting,
They grew enough to eat.

Back in ancient Egypt
What wondrous things they did.
To honor the great pharaohs,
They built pyramids.
The pyramids served as
The pharaohs' sacred tombs.
And all their royal treasures
Were kept in inner rooms.

Back in ancient Egypt
The people were advanced.
They created paper
From papyrus plants.
They wrote in hieroglyphics,
A writing done with art,
And invented a new calendar
To tell the months apart.

Mayas, Aztecs, and Incas

(sung to "London Bridge")

Three great Indian civilizations,
The Maya, Aztec, and Inca nations,
Each with widespread populations,
Three great Indian nations thrived.

Over three thousand years ago
The Mayas lived in Mexico.
They made fine art, and corn they'd grow.
Sing of the Maya Indians!

About six hundred years ago
The Aztecs ruled in Mexico.
They built great temples high and low.
Sing of the Aztec Indians!

About five hundred years ago
In South America, near Cuzco,
The Incas built roads to and fro.
Sing of the Inca Indians!

Native Americans

(sung to "The Alphabet Song")

A for Apache, B for Beaver,
C for Cherokee, all great achievers!

D for Dakota, E for Erie,
F for Fox, so brave and cheery!

G for Gulf, H for Hare,
I for Iroquois, oh what flair!

J for Jivaro, K for Kickapoo,
L for Lenape and Laguna, too.

M for Mohawk, N for Navajo,
O for Ottawa, Osage, and Oto.

P for Pueblo, Q for Quapaw,
R for Rumsen, oh what awe!

S for Shawnee, T for Tlingit,
U for Ute, for them we sing it!

V for Vaniuki, W for Wyandot,
X for Sioux (with X the end spot!)

Y for Yuma, Z for Zapotec,
Native Americans, people to respect!

The Pilgrims

(sung to "When Johnny Comes Marching Home")

The Pilgrims came to Plymouth Rock.
Hurrah! Hurrah!
In 1620 the *Mayflower* docked.
Hurrah! Hurrah!
The Pilgrims came to America's shore
To find the freedom they lacked before.
And heroic figures led the Pilgrims on.

William Bradford, brave was he.
Hurrah! Hurrah!
He led the Plymouth Colony.
Hurrah! Hurrah!
William Bradford showed the way
And held the first Thanksgiving Day.
This heroic figure led the Pilgrims on.

Miles Standish, he advised.
Hurrah! Hurrah!
Militia men he organized.
Hurrah! Hurrah!
Miles Standish, a bright young sir,
He served as colony treasurer.
This heroic figure led the Pilgrims on.

John Alden led the colony.
Hurrah! Hurrah!
Assistant governor was he.
Hurrah! Hurrah!
John Alden, very strong and stern,
He helped the Pilgrims survive and learn.
This heroic figure led the Pilgrims on.

Squanto helped the Pilgrims out.
Hurrah! Hurrah!
He got them through the snow and drought.
Hurrah! Hurrah!
Squanto taught them to plant and fish.
And keeping peace was his fervent wish.
This heroic figure led the Pilgrims on.

The 13 Original Colonies

(sung to "Ninety-Nine Bottles")

The 13 original colonies
In North America,
The colonists came
And staked their claim
In 13 original colonies.

New Hampshire, Connecticut, and Rhode Island,
Massachusetts, too.
These were New England colonies,
The 13 original colonies.

New York, New Jersey, Pennsylvania,
Maryland, Delaware, too.
These were the Middle colonies,
The 13 original colonies.

North Carolina, South Carolina,
Virginia, Georgia, too.
These were the Southern colonies,
The 13 original colonies.

The 13 original colonies
In North America,
The colonists came
And staked their claim
In 13 original colonies.

The American Revolution

(sung to "Yankee Doodle")

Back in 1775
There was a revolution.
American colonists fought against
Great Britain's persecution.

The Stamp Act taxed the colonists.
The Townshend Act did, too.
"Unfair!" the colonists boldly cried,
As their resentment grew.

The colonists weren't allowed to serve
As part of England's nation.
They argued, "Why should we be taxed
Without representation?"

"Tax their tea!" Great Britain ruled.
"No!" a plea came hearty.
The angry colonists dumped their tea
At the big Boston Tea Party.

At Lexington and Concord, Mass.
The rifles sounded gravely.
American minutemen battled
British redcoats very bravely.

Colonists rallied to the cause,
"Freedom!" was their cry.
Patriotic leaders rose
And swore, "It's do or die!"

Nathan Hale and Patrick Henry,
Benjamin Franklin, too;
Thomas Paine and Paul Revere,
All heroes tried and true.

General George Washington
Led with dedication;
And when the battles all were done,
The U.S. was a nation!

Scholastic Teaching Resources

The Declaration of Independence

(sung to "It Ain't Gonna Rain No More")

The Declaration of Independence,
What a grand decree!
Our Founding Fathers' document
Declaring that we all are free.

Thomas Jefferson penned the words
Of our philosophy:
All people are created equal,
All deserve their liberty!

Benjamin Franklin and John Adams
Formed a committee,
Guiding Jefferson in ideas
Declaring that we all are free.

The Declaration of Independence
Told to a large degree
How England had abused its power
And ruled its colonies unfairly!

The Declaration boldly stated
The necessity
To form a new nation and government
So colonists could live freely.

The Continental Congress voted
And they all agreed;
On July 4, 1776,
The U.S.A. came to be!

The Declaration of Independence,
What a grand decree!
Our Founding Fathers' document
Declaring that we all are free.

Westward Expansion

(sung to "Clementine")

Covered wagons headed westward,
Filled with settlers seeking land.
The Louisiana Purchase
Helped the U.S. to expand.

All throughout the 1800s
Blazing trails were headed west,
Santa Fe to San Francisco.
Pioneer life soon progressed.

Hail the heroes of expansion:
Davy Crockett, Daniel Boone.
Lewis and Clark's great expedition
Opened up the west so soon.

Past the Great Plains, past the Rockies,
Facing winters bitter cold,
Facing dust storms and tornadoes,
Staying brave and staying bold.

By the end of the 1860s
Locomotives rode the rail.
The Transcontinental Railroad
Spanned the country, bringing mail.

Covered wagons headed westward,
Filled with settlers seeking land.
Pioneers who headed westward
Helped our country to expand.

The Oregon Trail

(sung to "There's a Hole in the Bucket")

There's a road that I'm travelin',
Northwest out to Oregon.
There's a road that I'm travelin',
The Oregon Trail.

I started out from
Independence, Missouri.
It'll take me five months
To go two thousand miles.

I followed the trail
To Fort Kearny, Nebraska;
Then up the Platte River,
On the Oregon Trail.

Fort Laramie, Wyoming,
To Soda Springs, Idaho.
I crossed the Blue Mountains,
On the Oregon Trail.

From Walla Walla, Washington,
Down the Columbia River;
At last, Fort Vancouver,
On the Oregon Trail.

The Civil War

(sung to "The Battle Hymn of the Republic")

In 1861, our nation sadly disagreed.
The North said, "Slavery's something
That our country doesn't need."
The southern states grew angry
And they started to secede.
The Civil War began.

Chorus:
What a tragic situation,
Sadly splitting up our nation,
Leaving us in devastation,
That was the Civil War.

So many famous battles
Where so many soldiers fell:
Bull Run and then Antietam,
And at Gettysburg as well.
The burning of Atlanta
Was a sorry tale to tell.
The Civil War raged on.

Chorus

Now, President Abe Lincoln
Worked to keep the Union whole.
His Gettysburg Address
Addressed his dedicated goal
To guarantee equality
For every living soul
And end the Civil War.

Chorus

The Emancipation Proclamation
Said, "Southern slaves are free,"
And then at Appomattox
General Grant met General Lee.
The South surrendered to the North,
Which led to the decree:
The Civil War is done!

Chorus

50 States Join the Union

(sung to "You Are My Sunshine")

You should be well aware
The first state was Delaware,
The very first state in the U.S.A.
Then Pennsylvania,
New Jersey, Georgia,
Connecticut, Massachusetts came to stay.

Next was Maryland,
South Carolina,
New Hampshire, Virginia, and then New York;
North Carolina,
Rhode Island, Vermont,
Kentucky, and Tennessee came aboard.

Me, oh, my, oh!
Next came Ohio,
Louisiana, Indiana, Mississippi, too;
Illinois, Alabama,
Maine, and Missouri,
Arkansas, and Michigan joined the crew.

Florida, Texas,
Iowa, Wisconsin,
California, Minnesota, Oregon, then
Welcome to Kansas,
Then West Virginia,
Nevada, Nebraska all joined in.

Next, Colorado,
North Dakota, South Dakota,
Montana, Washington, Idaho, and
Wyoming, Utah, then Oklahoma,
And New Mexico joined the land.

Next, Arizona,
Then Alaska,
Finally Hawaii became a state.
Fifty states that
All are united,
United in a country mighty and great.

Women's Rights

(sung to "Goodnight, Ladies")

Chorus:
Special women,
Special women,
Special women,
You fought for women's rights.

Determined, how you rolled along,
Spoke out strong, led the throng.
Working hard to right each wrong,
You fought for women's rights.

Chorus

How you worked so tirelessly,
Susan B. Anthony,
Leading protests just to see
That women got the vote.

Elizabeth Cady Stanton, too.
Women owe lots to you.
At conferences, you shared your view
That women must have rights.

Chorus

Cheers go to Lucretia Mott,
For organizing quite a lot.
And, Lucy Stone, no one forgot
Your talks on women's rights.

Hooray for Carrie Chapman Catt.
Give a cheer! Tip your hat!
Celebrate the women that
Fought hard for women's rights!

Chorus

Civil Rights

(sung to "Do Your Ears Hang Low?")

Tell me, who fought the fights?
Who promoted civil rights?
Who devoted days and nights
Working hard for rights?
Who rose to the heights
In the struggle for rights,
For civil rights?

Harriet Tubman was brave,
Freeing many a slave.
The Underground Railroad
She helped to pave.
She risked her life
In order to save
People's civil rights!

Sojourner Truth, you see,
Opposed slavery.
This former slave
Spoke for equality.
Her message reached
The White House in D.C.
"We want civil rights!"

Frederick Douglass, so bright,
Was a true guiding light.
An important newspaper
He did write.
He urged his readers
All to unite
For civil rights!

Dr. Martin Luther King
Did many a great thing.
He preached and said,
"Let freedom ring!"
He marched to spread
His inspiring dream
Of civil rights!

Electing a President

(sung to "Oh, Dear, What Can the Matter Be?")

Chorus:
How do we get a president
Who will lead us in government?
When it comes to the president,
How is the office attained?

The process begins with lots of campaigning,
The candidates speak, with each one explaining
What they plan to do if they'll be maintaining
The head of our nation one day.

Chorus

Political parties each hold a convention
Where candidates' names get plenty of mention,
The delegates vote, and after much tension,
One candidate's chosen to run!

Chorus

Election Day comes, and in the election
The voters cast votes to make their selection,
Each state totals up in ballot collection
The votes that each candidate gets.

Chorus

The Electoral College meets some weeks later,
Each state's votes are cast, and once a collator
Has totaled the sum, the candidate greater
Is named as our next president!

Chorus

Scholastic Teaching Resources

U.S. Presidents

(sung to "The Muffin Man")

Do you know the presidents,
The presidents, the presidents?
Do you know the presidents
Who led the U.S.A.?

Washington was number one,
Then came Adams and Jefferson;
Madison, Monroe, and Adams' son.
All led the U.S.A.

Jackson, Van Buren, Harrison,
Tyler, Polk, and Taylor won;
Fillmore, Pierce, and Buchanan.
All led the U.S.A.

Lincoln, Johnson, Grant, and then
Hayes and Garfield, Arthur, then
Cleveland, Harrison, and Cleveland *again*!
They led the U.S.A.

McKinley, Roosevelt (Theodore),
Taft and Wilson. Wait! There's more.
Harding, Coolidge joined the corps.
They led the U.S.A.

Hoover, Roosevelt (Franklin D.),
Truman, Eisenhower, Kennedy,
Johnson, Nixon, Ford—proudly.
All led the U.S.A.

Carter, Reagan, Bush—all won,
Next was Clinton, then Bush's son.
Our presidents' list for now is done.
They led the U.S.A.

Three Branches of Government

(sung to "The Wheels on the Bus")

The three branches of government,
Government, government,
The three branches of government,
What does each one do?

The legislative branch creates our laws,
Writes new laws, passes laws.
Members of Congress make the laws,
Setting down the rules.

The executive branch enforces laws,
Carries out laws, applies the laws.
The president and police enforce the laws,
Making sure they're obeyed.

The judicial branch reviews the laws,
Rules on laws, interprets laws.
Courts and judges judge the laws,
Deciding if they're fair.

The three branches of government,
Government, government,
The three branches of government,
Each one has a special role.

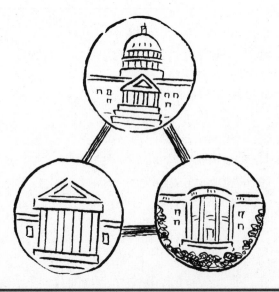

U.S. Regions

(sung to "This Land Is Your Land")

The U.S.A.
Is divided into regions,
Seven main regions
In the U.S.A.
New England, Mid Atlantic,
Southern, Midwestern,
Rocky Mountain, Southwestern,
Pacific Coast. Hey!

The New England states are:
Connecticut, Maine,
Massachusetts, New Hampshire,
Rhode Island, and Vermont.
The Mid Atlantic states are:
New York and New Jersey,
Plus Pennsylvania.
What more could you want?

The Southern states are:
Delaware, Florida,
Maryland, Kentucky,
Mississippi, Alabama,
Arkansas, Tennessee,
Virginia, West Virginia,
North Carolina, South Carolina,
Georgia, Louisiana.

The Midwestern states are:
Kansas, Nebraska,
Iowa, Illinois,
Ohio, Minnesota,
Michigan, Missouri,
Wisconsin, Indiana,
North Dakota,
And South Dakota.

The Rocky Mountain states are:
Idaho, Nevada,
Montana, Wyoming,
Utah, Colorado.
The Southwestern states are:
Texas, Arizona,
New Mexico and
Oklahoma.

The Pacific Coast states are:
California, Washington,
And then Oregon.
That's 48. Hey!
The last two states,
Alaska and Hawaii,
Are in other areas
Further away.

Times Zones

(sung to "Alouette")

Chorus:
Different times zones,
Many different time zones,
Different time zones
In the U.S.A.

Do you know the Eastern Time?
It's 6 p.m. in Eastern Time,
6 p.m. Eastern Time,
O-o-o-o-oh!

Chorus

Do you know the Central Time?
It's 5 p.m. in Central Time,
5 p.m. Central Time,
6 p.m. Eastern Time.
O-o-o-o-oh!

Chorus

Do you know the Mountain Time?
It's 4 p.m. in Mountain Time,
4 p.m. Mountain Time,
5 p.m. Central Time,
6 p.m. Eastern Time.
O-o-o-o-oh!

Chorus

Do you know Pacific Time?
It's 3 p.m. Pacific Time,
3 p.m. Pacific Time,
4 p.m. Mountain Time,
5 p.m. Central Time,
6 p.m. Eastern Time.
O-o-o-o-oh!

Chorus

Do you know Alaska Time?
It's 2 p.m. Alaska Time,
2 p.m. Alaska Time,
3 p.m. Pacific Time,
4 p.m. Mountain Time,
5 p.m. Central Time,
6 p.m. Eastern Time.
O-o-o-o-oh!

Chorus

Do you know Hawaii Time?
It's 1 p.m. Hawaii Time,
1 p.m. Hawaii Time,
2 p.m. Alaska Time,
3 p.m. Pacific Time,
4 p.m. Mountain Time,
5 p.m. Central Time,
6 p.m. Eastern Time.
O-o-o-o-oh!

Chorus

Five Great Lakes

(sung to "The Old Gray Mare")

The five Great Lakes
Are Erie and Michigan,
Huron, Superior.
Last is Ontario.
The five Great Lakes
Are easy to remember.
Just think of the key word *HOMES*.

Think of the key word *HOMES*,
Think of the key word *HOMES*.

The five Great Lakes:
The H is for Huron,
The O for Ontario,
The M is for Michigan.
The five Great Lakes:
The E is for Erie,
And S for Superior.

HOMES!

MATH & SCIENCE

Skip Counting

(sung to "Ninety-Nine Bottles")

Five numbers we skip at a time,
Five numbers we skip,
Yes, we can count a large amount
When five numbers we skip at a time.

5, 10, 15, 20,
25, 30, and more!
35, 40, 45, 50,
Five numbers we skip at a time!

Ten numbers we skip at a time,
Ten numbers we skip,
Yes, we can count a large amount
When ten numbers we skip at a time.

10, 20, 30, 40,
50, 60, and more!
70, 80, 90, 100,
Ten numbers we skip at a time!

One hundred numbers we skip at a time,
One hundred numbers we skip,
Yes, we can count a large amount
When one hundred numbers we skip at a time.
100, 200, 300, 400,
500, 600, and more!
700, 800, 900, 1000,
One hundred numbers we skip at a time!

Multiplication Facts

(sung to "Down by the Station")

Multiplication,
Multiplying numbers,
Multiplication,
A quick way to count!
Choose any number,
Then choose another,
Multiply the numbers
To find the amount.

Numbers 1 to 10
When multiplied by 2 are
2, 4, 6, 8, 10, and 12,
14, 16, 18, and 20.
Multiples of 2 are oh, so swell!

Numbers 1 to 10
When multiplied by 3 are
3, 6, 9, 12, 15, 18, 21,
24, 27, and then 30.
Multiples of 3 are extremely fun!

Numbers 1 to 10
When multiplied by 4 are
4, 8, 12, 16, 20, 24,
28, 32, 36, and 40.
Multiples of 4 are numbers to adore!

Numbers 1 to 10
When multiplied by 5 are
5, 10, 15, 20, 25,
30, 35, 40, 45, and 50.
Multiples of 5 really come alive!

Numbers 1 to 10
When multiplied by 6 are
6, 12, 18, 24, 30, 36,
42, 48, 54, and 60.
Multiples of 6 increase very quick!

Numbers 1 to 10
When multiplied by 7 are
7, 14, 21, 28, 35,
42, 49, 56, 63, 70.
Multiples of 7 really come alive!

Numbers 1 to 10
When multiplied by 8 are
8, 16, 24, 32, 40, 48,
56, 64, 72, and 80.
Multiples of 8 are truly great!

Numbers 1 to 10
When multiplied by 9 are
9, 18, 27, 36, 45,
54, 63, 72, 81, and 90.
Multiples of 9 really come alive!

Numbers 1 to 10
When multiplied by 10 are
10, 20, 30, 40, 50, 60, and
70, 80, 90, and finally 100.
Multiples of 10 are truly grand!

Money

(sung to "Miss Lucy")

Miss Lucy had a penny,
That means she had a cent.
She kept on saving pennies,
Then to the bank she went.

She traded in her pennies,
And got some nickels back.
She kept on saving nickels,
And piled them in a stack.

She traded in her nickels,
And she got back some dimes.
She saved more dimes and nickels
For some quarters over time.

She saved more quarters, saying,
"My pile still increases!"
Then she traded in her quarters
For some half-dollar pieces.

Miss Lucy kept on saving,
She saved some more until
She traded in her half dollars
For many dollar bills!

Miss Lucy learned a lesson,
A lesson good to know:
If you save up your money,
Then it will surely grow!

Weigh and Measure

(sung to "London Bridge")

Chorus:
Weigh and measure, oh what fun!
Oh what fun! Oh what fun!
Weigh and measure, oh what fun!
Weigh and measure!

Weigh the ounces, weigh the pounds,
Weigh the tons, weigh the tons!
Weigh the carats, weigh the grams,
Weigh and measure!

Chorus

Measure inches, measure feet,
Measure yards, oh how neat!
Measure meters, measure miles,
Weigh and measure!

Chorus

Measure pints and measure cups,
Measure quarts, add them up.
Measure gallons, measure liters,
Weigh and measure!

Chorus

Fractions

(sung to "When the Saints Go Marching In")

Oh, when a pizza's cut in half,
Oh, when a pizza's cut in half,
There are equal parts for two people,
When a pizza's cut in half.

Oh, when a pizza's cut in thirds,
Oh, when a pizza's cut in thirds,
There are equal parts for three people,
When a pizza's cut in thirds.

Oh, when a pizza's cut in fourths,
Oh, when a pizza's cut in fourths,
There are equal parts for four people,
When a pizza's cut in fourths.

Oh, when a pizza's cut in fifths,
Oh, when a pizza's cut in fifths,
There are equal parts for five people,
When a pizza's cut in fifths.

Oh, when a pizza's cut in sixths,
Oh, when a pizza's cut in sixths,
There are equal parts for six people,
When a pizza's cut in sixths.

Decimal Point

(sung to "Mary Had a Little Lamb")

Chorus:
Some numbers have a decimal point,
Decimal point, decimal point.
Some numbers have a decimal point
To show amounts in tenths.

2.1 is two and one tenth.
4.6 is four and six tenths.
8.8 is eight and eight tenths.
The decimal shows the tenths.

Chorus

0.3 is three tenths.
0.5 is five tenths.
0.7 is seven tenths.
The decimal shows the tenths.

Chorus

3.0 is three and no tenths.
6.0 is six and no tenths.
9.0 is nine and no tenths.
The decimal shows the tenths.

Chorus

Geometry Shapes

(sung to "London Bridge")

Geometry deals with different figures,
Sides and angles, shapes and figures.
What are the names of the different figures
That we find in geometry?

Triangle has three sides, three angles.
Quadrilateral has four sides, four angles.
Pentagon has five sides, five angles.
These are shapes in geometry.

Hexagon has six sides, six angles.
Heptagon has seven sides, seven angles.
Octagon has eight sides, eight angles.
These are shapes in geometry.

Nonagon has nine sides, nine angles.
Decagon has ten sides, ten angles.
Dodecagon has twelve sides, twelve angles.
These are shapes in geometry.

-Ology

(sung to "Little Brown Jug")

Chorus:
Science fields, A to Z,
Are labeled by their -ology.
You can earn a science degree
Studying an -ology.

Study life—biology,
Animals—zoology,
Past cultures—archaeology,
Fossils—paleontology.

Chorus

Study earth—geology,
Earthquakes—seismology,
Environment—ecology,
Weather—meteorology.

Chorus

Study birds—ornithology,
Reptiles—herpetology,
Insects—entomology,
Fish—ichthyology.

Chorus

Study mammals—mammalogy,
Humans—anthropology,
Behavior—psychology,
Society—sociology.

Chorus

Study disease—pathology,
Skin—dermatology,
Bones—osteology,
Bacteria—bacteriology.

Chorus

Study hearts—cardiology,
X-rays—radiology,
You will grow so "knowledge-y"
Studying an -ology.

Chorus

74

Scientific Classifications

(sung to "Bingo")

I know the system
Scientists use
To classify all life forms.

How they classify,
How they classify,
How they classify,
They classify all life forms:

Kingdom, phylum, class, order,
Family, genus, species.

That's how they classify,
That's how they classify,
That's how they classify,
They classify all life forms.

Let's see the system
Scientists use
To classify a lion:

Kingdom: Animalia,
Phylum: Chordata,
Class: Mammalia,
To classify a lion.
Order: Carnivora,
Family: Felidae,
Genus: Panthera,
To classify a lion.
Species: Leo,
That's how they classify,
That's how they classify,
They classify a lion!

Systems of the Human Body

(sung to "Hush, Little Baby")

The human body is made of a lot.
It runs on the many systems it's got.

The skeletal system consists of bones.
It forms a framework hard as stones.

The muscular system helps us to move.
Muscles allow our strength to improve.

The digestive system breaks down our food.
The stomach goes to work once the mouth has chewed.

The respiratory system lets us breathe.
Our lungs take in air, then let it leave.

The circulatory system carries our blood.
The heart, veins, and arteries handle the flood.

The excretory system removes our waste.
Our kidneys and colon make sure it's erased.

The reproductive system creates our young.
Giving parents a daughter or son.

The endocrine system consists of glands.
They help us cope with our growth demands.

The nervous system controls how we act.
Our brain and spinal cord keep behavior intact.

The immune system protects us from disease.
Our skin blocks germs from a cough or sneeze.

The human body is made of a lot.
It runs on the many systems it's got.

Skeletal System

(sung to "There's a Hole in the Bucket")

There are bones in our body,
The skeletal system.
There are bones in our body,
Over two hundred bones.

The cranium's the skull bone.
The hammer's the ear bone.
The nasal's the nose bone.
We have many bones.

The maxilla's the upper jaw.
The mandible's the lower jaw.
The zygoma's the cheekbone.
We have many bones.

The frontal's the forehead.
The clavicle's the collarbone.
The scapula's the shoulder blade.
We have many bones.

The sternum's the breastbone.
The vertebrae are spine bones.
The innominate's the hipbone.
We have many bones.

The femur's the thighbone.
The tibia's the shinbone.
The fibula's the calf bone.
We have many bones.

The humerus is the upper arm.
The radius is the main forearm.
The patella's the kneecap.
We have many bones.

The carpal's the wrist bone.
Metacarpals are hand bones.
Phalanges are finger bones.
We have many bones.

The tarsus are ankle bones.
Metatarsals are foot bones.
Phalanges are toe bones.
We have many bones.

There are bones in our body,
The skeletal system.
There are bones in our body,
Over two hundred bones.

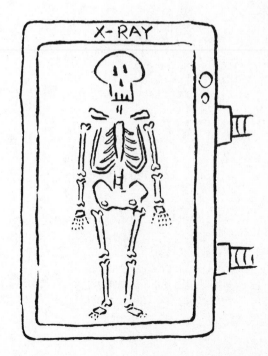

How the Heart Works

(sung to "Hokey Pokey")

The chambers on the right
Are busy pumping blood.
The chambers on the right
Pump blood to the lungs.
The carbon dioxide
In the blood is removed.
That's how the heart works out!

The chambers on the left
Are busy pumping blood.
The chambers on the left
Pump blood from the lungs.
They pump it to the body
With fresh oxygen.
That's how the heart works out!

The chambers on the left,
The chambers on the right,
The chambers of the heart
Pump blood day and night.
The atria and ventricles
Are pumping blood about.
That's how the heart works out!

Parts of the Brain

(sung to "Home on the Range")

The whole human brain
Has three parts that contain
Everything that you need for control.
Your brain helps you feel
And to learn a great deal
And to plan and accomplish a goal.

Chorus:
Three parts of the brain,
Every part has a job to attain.
The brain helps you act.
And it's also a fact,
It allows you to think and explain.

The cerebrum does much,
Sensing temperature and touch,
Sending signals to muscles as well.
It stores information
And promotes education,
By letting you speak, read, and spell.

Chorus

The cerebellum you'll find
In the back of your mind.
It controls every move that you make.
Your balance is fine.
And your posture's in line.
The cerebellum guides each step you take.

Chorus

The brain stem is key.
It controls how you breathe.
And it governs your heartbeat all right.
It helps move your eyes
And controls pupil size,
So you're able to see in all light.

Chorus

Mammals

(sung to "London Bridge")

Apes and bears and cats are mammals.
Sheep and deer and rats are mammals.
Goats and flying bats are mammals.
We are mammals, too!

Horses, zebras, hogs are mammals.
Porcupines and dogs are mammals.
Beavers gnawing logs are mammals.
We are mammals, too!

Cows and bulls and gnus are mammals.
Hopping kangaroos are mammals.
Elephants in zoos are mammals.
We are mammals, too!

Wolves that howl and cry are mammals.
Foxes oh so sly are mammals.
Hippopotami are mammals.
We are mammals, too!

Monkeys in a tree are mammals.
Dolphins in the sea are mammals.
Rabbits running free are mammals.
We are mammals, too!

All giraffes and mice are mammals.
Seals out on the ice are mammals.
Skunks who don't smell nice are mammals.
We are mammals, too!

Armadillos, they are mammals.
Squirrels at work and play are mammals.
Sloths that loaf all day are mammals.
We are mammals, too!

Lions, tigers, whales are mammals.
Pigs with curly tails are mammals.
What are camels? Also mammals.
We are mammals, too!

Fish

(sung to "When Johnny Comes Marching Home")

Fish are swimming in the sea.
Hurrah! Hurrah!
Through their gills, they're breathing free.
Hurrah! Hurrah!
Fish are swimming in the sea.
Their fins propel them steadily.
In different waters
Are different kinds of fish.

In coastal waters, look around!
Hurrah! Hurrah!
Cod and flounder can be found.
Hurrah! Hurrah!
Sea bass, marlins, tuna, too;
Barracudas and sharks in view.
In coastal waters
Are different kinds of fish.

In coral reefs, so much to see,
Hurrah! Hurrah!
The clownfish and anemone,
Hurrah! Hurrah!
Snapper, grouper, eel, of course;
Plus angelfish and the sea horse.
In coral reefs
Are different kinds of fish.

Deep in the ocean, let's explore,
Hurrah! Hurrah!
The halibut, hake, and much more.
Hurrah! Hurrah!
Lantern fish and anglers, too;
Vipers with sharp teeth to view.
In the ocean deep
Are different kinds of fish.

In temperate rivers, lakes, and streams,
Hurrah! Hurrah!
Carp and salmon can be seen.
Hurrah! Hurrah!
Sturgeon, perch, pike, and trout;
Whitefish also swim about.
In temperate waters
Are different kinds of fish.

Insects

(sung to "Camptown Races")

What are small and have six legs?
Insects! Insects!
Who may lay a lot of eggs?
Many insects do.

Whose antennae pick up sound?
Insects! Insects!
Who can fly or creep around?
Many insects do.

Chorus:
Moths and ants and flies,
Ladybugs and bees,
Butterflies and katydids,
Grasshoppers and fleas.

What have an exoskeleton?
Insects! Insects!
A head, thorax, and abdomen?
Many insects do.

What are there millions of?
Insects! Insects!
Who crawls low and flies above?
Many insects do.

Chorus

Birds and Their Habitats

(sung to "Ninety-Nine Bottles")

Hundreds of birds are all around,
Hundreds of birds to see.
You can find all different kinds,
Hundreds of birds are all around.

In urban settings, robins fly,
Cardinals, sparrows, too.
Jays and mockingbirds sing their sound,
Hundreds of birds are all around.

In forests and woodlands, cuckoos live,
Warblers and wrens as well.
Orioles chirp. Woodpeckers pound.
Hundreds of birds are all around.

In grasslands, meadowlarks share their song.
Flycatchers catch their flies.
Kingbirds and owls abound.
Hundreds of birds are all around.

In deserts, golden eagles sail.
Vultures also fly.
Roadrunners and quail are found.
Hundreds of birds are all around.

In marshes and in inland waters,
Loons and ducks all swim.
Herons and storks wade near ground.
Hundreds of birds are all around.

Hundreds of birds are all around,
Hundreds of birds to see.
You can find all different kinds,
Hundreds of birds are all around.

Reptiles

(sung to "Pop! Goes the Weasel")

All around a desert or beach,
You may see a reptile,
A turtle, tortoise, lizard, or snake.
Yep! That's a reptile!

Look for skin that's scaly and dry.
That's a sign of reptiles.
Does it breathe the air with lungs?
Yep! That's a reptile!

All around a marshland or swamp,
You may see a reptile,
An alligator or crocodile.
Yep! That's a reptile!

Is the creature cold-blooded, too?
That's a sign of reptiles.
Some say even dinosaurs.
Yep! They were reptiles!

Amphibians

(sung to "Miss Lucy")

If you see salamanders,
If you see toads or frogs,
Then you have seen amphibians
In streams, in ponds, or logs.

They live part-time in water.
They live part-time on land.
They swim in lakes and puddles.
They move on grass and sand.

Their skin is moist and scaleless.
They creep on tiny legs.
They find a stream or puddle,
And there they lay their eggs.

Caecilians are amphibians
Who have no legs at all.
They look just like an earthworm.
To travel, they must crawl.

Amphibians are creatures,
In water or on land.
They swim in lakes and puddles.
They move on grass and sand.

Parts of a Plant

(sung to "The Muffin Man")

Chorus:
Do you know the different parts,
The different parts, the different parts.
Do you know the different parts
That make up a green plant?

Roots are growing underground.
They hold the plant safe and sound.
Water and minerals in the ground
Are soaked up by the roots.

Chorus

Stems hold leaves up to the light.
They carry water and food all right.
Some stems store food at the site
Where minerals may be kept.

Chorus

Leaves are a plant's food factory.
Chlorophyll gets light energy,
Mixed with water and air, you see.
Leaves make food for plants.

Chorus

Flowers grow the seeds that shoot.
A flower has parts that may include:
Petal, stamen, pistil, anther, fruit,
They help the seeds to grow.

Chorus

Seeds help plants to reproduce.
Seeds first grow and then come loose.
They germinate and introduce
A brand-new, live green plant!

Chorus

Photosynthesis

(sung to "Twinkle, Twinkle, Little Star")

Photosynthesis
What does it mean?
The way food is made
By plants that are green.
Leaves take in carbon dioxide
From the air.
Roots take in water
From soil down there.
The carbon dioxide and water
Must combine.
To make that happen
Requires sunshine.

Photosynthesis
What next is done?
Chlorophyll in leaves
Soaks up light from the sun.
Light provides energy
In order to combine
Carbon dioxide and water
Just fine.
The mixture makes sugar.
And wouldn't you know,
That's the food
A plant needs to grow.

Landforms

(sung to "This Land Is Your Land")

Chorus:
Our land has landforms,
Or special features.
This land is home to
So many creatures.
All kinds of landforms
Are found around the world.
Landforms make up our special land!

Up in the highlands,
You'll find the mountains,
Plus hills and cliffs,
And flat-top mesas.
These lands are highlands,
A special feature.
Landforms make up our special land!

Chorus

Down in the lowlands,
You'll find the canyons,
Plus river valleys,
And bluffs and gorges.
These lands are lowlands,
A special feature.
Landforms make up our special land!

Chorus

Deep in the wetlands
Are swamps and marshes,
Plus soggy bogs
With lots of water.
These lands are wetlands,
A special feature.
Landforms make up our special land!

Chorus

Across the plains
It's mostly treeless.
The land is flat
With grasses growing.
These lands are plains,
A special feature.
Landforms make up our special land!

Chorus

Four Layers of Earth

(sung to "Three Blind Mice")

Four layers of earth, four layers of earth.
The crust is first. The crust is first.
The crust is the surface, solid and thin.
The crust is called the earth's "skin."
Dig the earth to twenty miles in!
That's the crust.

Four layers of earth, four layers of earth.
The mantle is next. The mantle is next.
Under the crust, the mantle lies.
It's very hot, where rock really fries.
Dig one thousand eight hundred miles!
That's the mantle.

Four layers of earth, four layers of earth.
The outer core is third. The outer core is third.
Under the mantle, the outer core lies.
It's very hot, where rock really fries.
Dig three thousand two hundred miles!
That's the outer core.

Four layers of earth, four layers of earth.
The inner core is fourth. The inner core is fourth.
Under the outer, the inner core lies.
It's very hot, where rock really fries.
Dig in the earth four thousand miles!
That's the inner core.

Types of Clouds

(sung to "The Wheels on the Bus")

Chorus:
The sky has many types of clouds,
Types of clouds, types of clouds.
The sky has many types of clouds,
Classified by height.

Stratus clouds are low and gray,
Sheetlike clouds producing rain.
Stratocumulus are much the same,
Low, dark, heavy clouds.

Cumulus clouds are also low,
White and piled-up, you know.
Cumulonimbus are very low.
They bring heavy showers.

Chorus

Altostratus are grayish sheets,
Up six thousand to twenty thousand feet.
Altocumulus look so neat,
Fleecy bands in blue sky.

Cirrus clouds are way up high,
Twenty thousand to forty thousand feet in the sky.
Wispy clouds with crystals of ice,
Those are cirrus clouds.

Cirrostratus are just as high,
Milky, thin clouds in the sky.
Cirrocumulus are thin cloud lines
With ripples on their edges.

Chorus

Water Cycle

(sung to "You Are My Sunshine")

It starts with sunshine,
With lots of sunshine,
Shining on oceans,
Rivers and lakes.
The water's heated
By all the sunshine
And evaporates
As it bakes.

The water now turns
Into a vapor.
The vapor rises
Into the air.
The vapor cools off
And then condenses,
Forming water drops
In clouds up there.

The water drops are
A form of moisture.
Precipitation
Is what it's called.
In time the droplets
Fall back to earth, and
That's when rain, rain, rain
Starts to fall.

The water cycle's
An endless cycle.
It keeps repeating
Year after year.
The water rises
And vaporizes.
Then it comes down
Through the atmosphere.

Layers of the Atmosphere

(sung to "Mary Had a Little Lamb")

Layers of the atmosphere,
Atmosphere, atmosphere,
Layers of the atmosphere,
The air surrounding earth.

The troposphere is twelve miles high.
Dust and clouds are floating by.
Gas and vapor are in supply
In the troposphere.

The stratosphere is thirty miles high.
Icy winds are blowing by.
The air is very clear and dry
In the stratosphere.

The mesosphere is fifty miles high.
Temperatures get cold, no lie!
Minus one hundred degrees Fahrenheit
In the mesosphere.

The exosphere is three hundred ten miles high,
Separating earth and space, oh my!
Satellites are passing by
In the exosphere.

The thermosphere is four hundred miles high.
Electrical ions are in supply.
Radio waves and beams bounce by
In the thermosphere.

Light

(sung to "My Bonnie Lies Over the Ocean")

Light travels as swift as an arrow.
Light travels in only straight lines.
Light travels and bounces off surfaces,
Reflecting light into your eyes.

Light reflection,
Reflecting light into your eyes,
Your eyes.
Light reflection,
Reflecting light into your eyes.

Light travels through air very quickly,
But slower through water or glass.
Traveling from one to another,
The light seems to bend, or refract.

Light refraction,
The light seems to bend,
Or refract, refract.
Light refraction,
The light seems to bend, or refract.

Sound

(sung to "London Bridge")

Anything you hear is sound,
Any noise that's around.
Anything you hear is sound
On your eardrum.

Sound is just vibrating air,
Moving here, moving there.
Sound is just vibrating air
On your eardrum.

Frequency tells you the rate
At which sound will vibrate.
Fast or slow, it will vibrate
On your eardrum.

Pitch tells you the frequency.
High or low is the key.
More vibrations raise the key
On your eardrum.

Loudness is intensity,
Just how loud sound will be.
How many decibels it will be
On your eardrum.

Matter

(sung to "Oh, Dear, What Can the Matter Be?")

Chorus:
Tell me, what can matter be?
Is it anything I can see?
Tell me, what can matter be?
Something that occupies space.

Rocks are matter known as a solid.
Water is matter known as a liquid.
Air is matter known as a gas.
Yes, matter has three different forms.

Chorus

The smallest amount of matter's an atom.
When atoms combine, they form a molecule.
When molecules combine, they form a compound,
And matter is what they all are.

Chorus

Planets in the Solar System

(sung to "Down by the Station")

Our solar system
Has a lot of planets,
Eight different planets
Distant from the sun.
Here are the names of
All the different planets,
Listed in order of
Closeness to the sun:

First is Mercury,
Next comes Venus,
Followed by Earth,
Then Mars and Jupiter,
Saturn, Uranus,
And finally Neptune,
That is the order
Seen by astronomers!

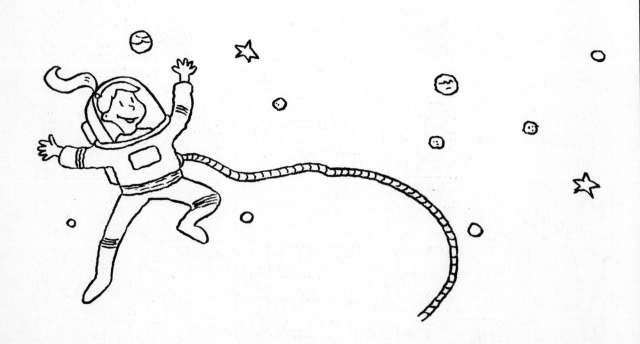